Contrary Collisions

A Journey through Paradoxes and
Balance

Pretty Jemima

BookLeaf
Publishing

India | USA | UK

Dedication

Dedicated to those who seek deeper understanding beyond life's simple terms.

Shout-outs

Special thanks to Merc and Meks for stopping by on journeys both old and new, and handing me moments for inspiration.

A heartfelt shout-out to Nands and Clev for your unwavering support through every shade of creativity and aspiration.

And to Kar, Babu, Selu, Ravs, KK, FKers, WTC Youth Guild and all the ones I can't name—you've been my cheer, my chaos, my motivation. Your belief in me is a blessing I hold with admiration. This one's for you, with love and appreciation!

Acknowledgements

First and foremost, I give thanks to God, the source of all inspiration, wisdom and creativity. Without His guidance, this collection would not have come to life. It is through His grace that the words flowed and the opposites collided, bringing forth new understanding.

I owe a deep sense of gratitude to my family and friends, whose unwavering support has been the foundation upon which this book was built. Your faith in me is a constant source of strength.

A special thank you to my editor, Nanditha Murali, whose keen eye and thoughtful suggestions helped shape these poems into their final form. I'm grateful for your enriching insights on poetry, art and life.

Heartfelt gratitude to the cover designer, Clevin Wilfred Rodrigues, for your exceptional artistry and vision in personalising and crafting a cover that perfectly captures the essence of this book.

To the teachers, mentors, poets and dear friends who have guided me along in life's creative journey, your wisdom has been my source of inspiration. You've shown me the power of words to explore, challenge and connect.

To my readers – past, present and future – thank you for your curiosity, your willingness to engage with the tensions between these opposites and your capacity for reflection. Your engagement with this work is what breathes life into it.

Finally, I want to acknowledge the beautiful collisions of thoughts, ideas and experiences that have led me here – those moments when opposing forces created something new. This book is as much yours as it is mine.

Preface

Contrary Collisions is an exploration of the tension between opposing forces that shape our world – forces that seem to stand at odds with each other, yet are inextricably intertwined. From the delicate balance of wisdom and knowledge to the transformative dance between creation and destruction, the poems in this collection are reflections on how opposites can clash and, ultimately, coexist to form the intricate tapestry of life.

This collection invites readers to reflect on the dualities that define our existence. Each poem serves as a mirror, inviting you to consider how opposing forces shape not only the world around you but also your inner journey. It is through these contrasts – order and chaos, dreams and reality, sanity and insanity – that we come to understand the beauty of balance and the necessity of change. Patterns that are similar, contrary and intricate – together touching every aspect of life – reverberate like lessons hidden in plain sight.

As you delve into these poems, you may recognise parts of yourself in their verses, finding comfort in their contradictions or sparking new perspectives on long-held beliefs. This is a book not of answers but of questions – questions that challenge the assumptions we hold about the world and ourselves.

The collision of opposites can be jarring, uncomfortable, even chaotic – but in that very clash, new possibilities emerge and old truths are transformed. May Contrary Collisions help you see the world not as a series of binary choices, but as a spectrum of moments where contrasts converge and create something more profound. The poems are written in an ascending sequence, simple dualities to start with and then to delve deeper into their journeys. Poems eleven to twenty are structured in a way where each opposing concept is explored individually before being woven together in a unifying passage. Oh! And do enjoy the illustrations along the way.

Welcome to this exploration of dualities. Let us walk together through this collision of opposites, seeking a deeper understanding of what it means to exist in a world defined by contradictions.

Table of Content

ENTANGLED REFLECTIONS

Sun and Moon

A bright morning champion, an ethereal
night companion,
Placed in a proximity of light years – a cosmic
canyon.
Each orbit spins a tale of love bittersweet,
Awaiting those rare, destined days,
When they draw near in celestial haze;
The Moon meets the shadow of the Earth,
dark and deep–
A fleeting kiss with the Sun eclipsed in a
shadowed sweep.
Revelling in the joy of exerting influence,
creating a rhythmic balance,
Governing the cosmic flow of natural cycles
with great forbearance.

The ill-fated lovers, each day they meet, yet
never embrace.
A distant handshake without a touch, like a
game of double Dutch.
For complementary is their love language;
Day shift to night shift, like a modern
marriage.

Light and Shadow

I spy with my eye a light so bright,
I spy with my eye grey whispers softening white.
A spectrum of colours I am, with a greyed-out
friend always in sight.
Basking in the views of all hues of my companion,
I'm the echo of light.
Through night or day, I remain in sight, but
my friend fades when the light is too bright.
Travel everywhere with my companion, I do,
playing with shapes as I skew.
I'm the sun's bright face,
And I, the quiet twin,
Forever linked, like the notes of the same
hymn.

Silence and Sound

In the art of sound, I find a quiet that sings,
A reminiscence of melody and rhythm it brings.
As various elements of expression resound,
Waves of cadence carrying emotion, my heart they surround.
I sit in absolute silence, yet filled with constant melodies–
The clash of voices in crescendo and calm; my healing remedy.
Two notes apart, yet in the same hold, they unfold.
The anticipation for both resonates in diction mighty & bold.

While the scales of sound belt tunes of rock,
my silence harmonises in blues.
What a pair, what an ensemble; in waves of
vibrato and straight tones,
In solo and in choir, in rhythms to modulate,
In compositions to accompany, in altos &
tenors to deduce;
In silence and sound, time and time again I
choose.

Love and Hate

As she sat in her usual corner with glasses on,
reading her verses,
I stood watching her, holding a soft memory
and a sharp ache in my pages.
As a rose that blooms and bleeds in the same
breath, I wondered of life and death.
Caught between grace and spite, I linger on
the edge, recalling the divine fondness in my
pledge.
As love and hate took the floor to battle,
unprocessed emotions; my soul rattled.
I flipped through my past, re-examining every
experience, learning new patterns and
perceptions, turning my love into hate and
her hate into love.
And suddenly they were more interwoven
than I thought they were, imprinted on each
other in past, present and future.
New forms of love held my hands softly, while
new forms of hate gripped it tight.
Fearful nostalgia turned down its shades of
fright, while memories of harsh words showed
a new side.

As extreme forms of love and hate turned
into each other, they pulled, pushed and
glitched like a stutter.
As high-voltage sparks of love broke through
heavily cemented Jericho walls of hate, it
swayed me into various emotional states.
Hate crumbled while retreating to whatever
shelter it could take; love marched through
the rubble, pronouncing the arrival of fate.
With a loud sigh and a tear in the eye, it
surveyed the ashes and aftermath, looking for
a clean slate.

Fire and Water

How fascinating to experience the
extraordinary; how fascinating to see
opposites collide.
The magnificence of burning fire caught in
the sparkling lapels of waves.
Two elements, fundamentally set apart, now
dance together, astounding unity in
reflections – each that moves to its own tune,
now caught in a serendipitous moment.
Where fire meets the tempest, the flames bow
to the waves, and where the intensity of heat
charges, the ripples of water concede.
In the language of fire and water, an uproar is
essential, but silence is the only truce. As
every molecule of oxygen is smothered to be
extinguished, a myriad of mirroring moments
comes to mind:
A camera capturing motion in stillness, two
opposing movements, in the eye of a lens
caught and frozen, a mind battling the
rational and irrational, two magnets
attracting each other with invisible force, two
souls oppositely aligned, falling in love –

opposites in rare unity like fiery heat and a
cooling wash.
Known to be set apart, yet brought together
by unforeseen forces.
The sizzle of a meet, the hiss of a reaction,
The swirling mist, a cooling embrace–
All caught in an elusive trace.

Roots and Wings

On a cold winter night, in the comfort of my
pillow and quilt, I lay, as the soft breeze of
dreams brought me into a hazy summer's
day...
I stood towering over the mass of green
around me as a strong tree, my roots digging
deep into the earth, my adornments
branching out for freedom to perch.
Anchored and mighty was the beauty I held,
and yet, still gazing upon the flutter of wings
with jealousy and want, I swelled.

In a misty moment, my dreamy view
transformed, my body grew lighter, my sight
sharper. I soared through clouds, a mighty
bird, devouring every sight beneath me. The
air, encircling, wrapped me with its force. My
flaps outstretched their true power.
As I glided on, a sudden urge to rest took
over me; I scanned the horizon, looking to
land on the tallest tree. As I descended down,
a familiar sight of mighty branches and lush
green leaves captured me. All the freedom
and flight I held, and yet, gazing upon the
majesty of anchored grounding, I swelled.

When I woke, I let the experience engulf me,
my roots soaked in the wisdom of ages, my
wings enthralled by unknown thrills of
changes. For roots are what keep me
grounded and wise like the sages, and wings
keep me soaring while seeking new places.
Rooted yet in flight, one without the other is
only half a dream – with a startle, I realised.

Time and Timelessness

Some moments echo longer than a lifetime,
stretching into the eternal.
Some pass away like a gust of wind, leaving
nothing of substance.
And some stay lingering like a persistent
presence.

Time: a constant mystery–
An invisible force that runs the rhythm of
humanity; seen yet unseen.

Quiet yet loud, subtle yet unstoppable.
Oh, how moments pocket into time like a
beautifully crafted dim sum!
Every second, every minute and every hour
collecting parcels of flavoursome, bite-sized,
succulent treasures–
Some with a lasting and lingering taste, some
lost in the pot or leaving palates in haste.

Timelessness: moments so profound they
escape the restraints of a clock.
Ironically fully present, moments bubbling in
plain sight like a reminiscent bowl of
sambhar, filled with the taste of a thousand
emotions and a simple mixture of masalas.
A timeless taste of earthy, delectable lentils;
momentary collections of a comforting stew
that's supplemental.

The polarities of a lifetime, intertwined with
experiences, feelings, memories, tastes;
intertwined with people.
An infinite number of paradoxes strung on
the cords of a vast timeline–

A compounded structure existing in a
symbiotic alliance.
Infinite yet little,
Limited yet boundless,
Swift yet gradual,
Perceived yet unperceived.

The City and the Forest

The sounds of car honks on the street,
contrasting birds chirping in the tree;
The loud rhythmic hum of traffic cascading
into the gentle sound of the stream like
magic.
The city ends where the forest begins, and
their whispers collide – one a crowded
silence, another a murmur of solitude.

In the city's chaotic moments of a railway
crossing opening its gates, as people merged
and whizzed past each other in a narrow
space, life around me stilled and transported
into a pocket space where I heard the stillness
of nature's trails, the rustling of trees – both
carrying the echoes of life like bees.

In the forest's dense thicket of undergrowth,
exploring & stumbling upon a secret passage
the great green hid, taking jagged steps of
utter silence as the sky above changed its hues
in vibrance. In this silence I was transported
to hear the whispers and shadows of an

alleyway as cars in the near distance revved
their engines – both carrying the echoes of
mystery and vengeance.
Skyscrapers stand tall like trees, silent
witnesses to the passing of generations.
Neon signs light up like stars in the night sky,
a testament to light after dark.
For the city ends where the forest begins.

Stone and Feather

A heart of stone and a mind that floats free,
One choosing to live in pure agony, and one
choosing to flee.
What's carved in stone could not be softened
by the touch of a feather;
The transient mind could not touch the caged
heart – they remained untethered.
Fragility knocked and knocked, but resilience
would not respond.
A shield meant for protection fused in place,
refusing to leave,
A dream meant to soar, struggling daily to
breathe.
Pathways turned barriers, and barriers turned
pathways,
While gravity and flight battled endlessly.
Every day I grappled – a heart of stone, a
mind that floats free.

Known and Unknown

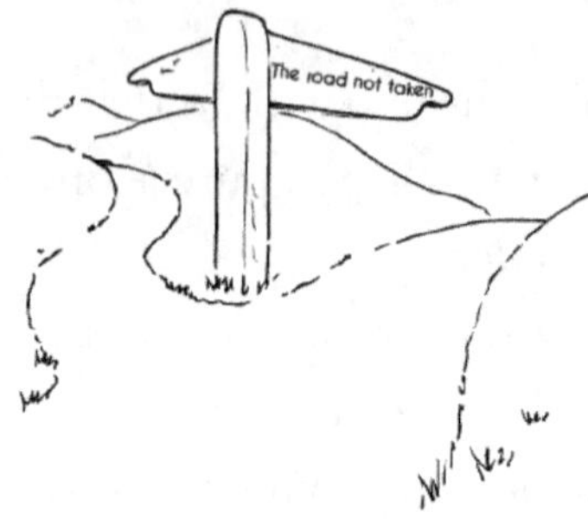

What would you choose?
A familiar path or a mysterious cruise?
For in the known lies comfort, like the
warmth of a winter quilt,
And in the unknown lies curiosity, like the
adventurous feeling of travelling.
In this map called life, strung with certainty
& uncertainty at hand,
Tried and tested, or possibilities unseen, each
path a test of affinity.
So, what would you choose?
An anchored ship or boundless sea? Stability
or possibility?
When two roads diverge in yellow woods,
would you be Frost

And take the one less travelled?
For in his timeless contemplation, he says it
made all the difference.
To most, known is their greatest purpose; to
some, unknown, an inescapable destiny.
Known or unknown, both produce a
much-needed perseverance.
Known or unknown, choose, for you are made
with purpose and divine significance.
Known or unknown, let your path be guided
by lights of intelligence.

PARALLEL REALMS

Dreams

In the quiet depth of sleep, I climb mountains
touched by the warmth of morning light; in
the soft, pillowy clouds of possibilities, my
vision takes sight.
An intangible canvas of desires, like savouring
a ripe custard apple bite,
I soar on a weightless high, diving into
unexplored worlds, as whispers of ambitions
take flight in colours oh so bright! With
luminous tenacity that just felt right.
I jump on stars, skip around cosmic sights,
touching the veil of fabric the universe makes,
coloured yet white.
Gleaming treasures and worlds I stroll
through – did I create this with my might?
Pathways and skies bend into shapes of
different heights.
As layers of misty worlds pass by, I catch a
glimpse of a metal top that won't stop,
spinning round and round under a streetlight.
And suddenly, the worlds freeze as my eyes
open wide,

But everything around me remains the same
sight.
Wait, where am I?

Reality

To the sound of distant church bells, my bare feet wandered on the cold floor, taking in the raw, sweet and intoxicating aroma of ginger chai waiting to be poured.

As snippets of last night's dream flashed through my mind – something about stars, custard apples and a spinning top – I shook my sleepiness away, thinking, 'What a dreamy score'.

As the morning's cold air seeped in through the window, I felt the weight of the day awaiting its chore.

Up and ready, fresh and out the door, the shift of bright heat and thick chemical air drove me for more; anchored by gravity, I moved through my everyday routine like a body working its core.

And suddenly, the grind had my power walks turn sluggish, like a muscle sore.

The taste of my double-cheese sandwich felt like another bore.

I took a walk onto a different lane for new sights to behold; I looked around at the

busyness of life on this new street. Wait, is
that the same shop as before?
Life whizzed past me like a European bus
tour.
I pulled out the metal top from my pocket
and spun it, just to be sure.
It spun a few times and fell in all its grandeur.
Suddenly, I felt the hollow ache of something
missing deep in my bones,
Like a beach without a shore. Like a room full
of possibilities without a door.
Is there a matter here of significance I should
know?

Intersection

If reality is the soil we walk upon, dreams
must be the cross-training shoes to put on.
For dreams without the grounding of reality
are a lost cause, and reality without unfurling
dreams is running life on pause.
Brick by brick, we build this life in certainty
and doubt. As my favourite band, Paramore,
says, 'Keep your feet on the ground when your
head's in the clouds'.

Power

Relentless and unyielding, like the surge of a
tidal wave,
The weight of its force can only be borne by
the mighty or the brave.
With a sweep of a hand, it builds empires; in
the wake of its footprints, it breaks them
down to ashes.
They say a golden crown weighs heavier than
stone,
Its shine blinding the bearer into an isolation
zone.
Like a spark in the mind that turns embers
into wildfire – a roaring upstart,
But like unchecked flames carried by wind, it
tears the world apart.
Hands meant to love, tend and create now
hold sceptres,
What was meant to strengthen, heal and
inspire, in some hands, becomes a broken
fender.
Yet, the same source that rises from within
helps in shaping prominent decisions,
enriching every day with its significant

provisions. Intrinsically sowed in all of us, waiting to be watered and grow with no restrictions. Is that when it truly loses its diligence?
For what is invoked in every strong moment and action is too much to bear for some factions. Losing its purpose and charm in unwarranted reactions.
As too much power tilts the cosmic scale like a poorly held chord,
It's obvious: we are but clay vessels, meant to pour, not to hoard.

Weakness

It stands like a glass on the edge, trembling in
its transparency,
With cracks that catch light – a mere whisper,
it would shatter. But, oh!
How it shines in its vulnerability.
Like delicate threads of a worn-out tapestry,
its true strength shines through all its glory–
Barely holding on, yet binding together a
whole story.
Like a quiet and steady ember, to the one who
endures, grace is ensured.
For in our incapacity, we are taught true
tenacity.
We paint shades of pride, only to learn
through humility,
In paradoxical lessons where defeat leads to
ultimate victory,
Where suffering in silence breeds strength
through misery.
Like a warrior and a servant sharing the same
Achilles' heel,
Or like a dandelion, thrown into the wind
like a fruit peel.

Weaknesses are the only things that reveal our
true place in the world,
For without them, some are lost in the whirl.

Intersection

Power is lightning – strikes fast and bright,
but fades away quickly.
Weakness lingers in the shadows, shaping
actions quietly.
Power is iron – strong and unyielding, but
brittle under pressure.
Weakness is silk – soft, yet it weaves
unbreakable bonds of treasure.
For one without the other is a wasted
measure.
Power is meant to be an armour that shields
from everything, like a soldier on the
battlefield protected by much more than his
own skill and training.
While weakness is like skin—vulnerable in
dangerous environments, yet the strongest
barrier of the body that protects all that is
within.

Sanity

A steady rhythm, mirroring my heartbeat like
a metronome,
Every thought and action guided by
coherence – like the codes written within
centrosomes.
In the inner compass that points north, life's
pathway unfolds like a honeycomb,
My voice of reason counsels, echoing an order
soaked in knowledge passed on like a hidden
tomb.
In this framework of a shared reality, my
measured thoughts find vitality.
I hunger to be held here and only here, for in
this functional stability, there is sheer clarity.
But why does this predictability not feel
broad enough?
In society's standards of behaviour and logic, I
feel handcuffed.
Why do the walls of steadiness move in closer
than outer? In discerning ability, it feels like
finding an expired voucher.
Why do the borders of sanity close in on me?
Is it to see clearly – or just merely?

Insanity

In the kaleidoscope of my shattered chaos,
each shard reflects an infinite reality.
In unravelling, there is a myriad of great
intelligence surrounded by losing coherence –
a great fatality.
My inner voice talks over itself, grabbing
every possible thought it can,
Flailing its loudness in the blaze of a distorted
plan.
In the face of fire in winter, blazing where it
shouldn't but illuminating what others
cannot see,
I ran and ran to get as far away as I could, yet
I circled back to the same raging plea.
Why must greatness meld into the loss of
reality's boundaries?
Why must there be such extremes to be felt to
dive into mysteries?
Why must unbound creativity only be shaped
by hurricanes,
And new perspectives seen as a delusional
difference?
Is this a standard or a state of mind?

For I hate to bind what's meant to be mined.

35

Intersection

In the very dogmas of sanity and insanity lie
reality and perception, both worlds playing
on interpretation – one aligns, while the
other diverges.
In the battle of control and surrender, both
seek equilibrium – one stays in, and the other
emerges.
In these neighbouring states that share a thin
line of boundary,
A shared living to some is contrary, but to
others, a necessity.
Like a final witness, from the notes of Fyodor
Dostoevsky:
'To be conscious is an illness—a real
thorough-going illness'.
Travelling between these walls feels like the
pangs of an extreme sport, like live, raw
power waiting to be harnessed, a few seconds
of blur it takes to re-adjust while going back
and forth like the photoreceptors in my eyes
adjusting themselves in the presence and
absence of light, cones to rods and rods to

cones.

Knowledge

To wisdom, my good old friend,
How do I scatter truth and yet not piece it
together?
How am I filled with substance yet lack
application?
How am I preserved, yet broken down in
chances of rot?
How do I inflate with pride, yet cower before
humility?
I gather the richness of discretion, and yet
prudence slips through my fingers.
I aim with precision like no other but find no
target to capture.
I count every second, not perceiving why.
I speak every syllable with certainty, but the
silence around me just dies.
They say to gain you, I must forget everything
I know – is this truth or a lie?
I gather power like a storm, unable to acquire
calm.
I gather all tools in abundance but lose myself
in the ideas of what to create.

I see all details with clarity, but what do they
mean? If I'm the palette full of colours,
shouldn't I be seen?
I hold all precious treasures with no means to
find a key.
Will you relieve me?

Wisdom

To knowledge, my brilliant youngin,
You are the seed meant to be scattered, but
only I know where it takes root.
You were made to be filled with every
necessary substance, but the power of
application is my sustenance.
You are preserved well for me to unlock your
potential. You possess discretion, but I dwell
with prudence.
The more you know, the more pride flows –
but don't worry, you don't know how little we
know.
Take your aim; I won't let you go astray.
Every second counts because they are
significant moments on display.
You have to listen to truly speak; you cannot
harness storms without consulting peace.
And truth it is: to attain me, you must cease.
You gather; I create.
Be my vision, and I'll help you interpret.
Be my palette, and with my artistry, I'll make
you seen.
Hold the treasure tight, for I hold the key.

For without you, there is no me. And without
my aid, you will be shaped into every form of
weapon there is to see.
I will relieve you if you choose to hold me
free.

Intersection

In his proverbs, the wise King Solomon writes, 'By wisdom, a house is built; through understanding, it is established; through knowledge, its rooms are filled with rare and beautiful treasures'.
While wisdom is required to create, knowledge is needed to enrich and satiate.
While knowledge is the map, wisdom experiences the journey.
Knowledge is light, and wisdom the prism; together, they refract to reveal colours of hidden exoticism. By wisdom, Earth's foundations were laid, and through knowledge, watery depths were divided.
Both gifts, divine in nature, are like a river and a raft.
They navigate through philosophy and curiosity, revealing the limitations of the human mind and pointing toward sovereignty.

Creation

A universal reaction, a cosmic reverberation that said, 'Let there be'– and just like that, a flame was born in the void, casting life into existence for all to see.

While sculpted stars and planets rose from the dust of powerful frequencies in inaudible silence, each took its designated place in cosmic exuberance.

Every breath, an echo of eternity's beginning; every rhythm, an endless waltz of becoming.

Ever since, a rapid song of change has taken form as reactions.

Anabolism – the constructive aspect of metabolism.

Like an architect's blueprint, it stitches together fragments of possibility: scattered atoms into structures of life, threads of DNA into forms of expression.

Every cell it divides is like an artist's hand, carving mountains from stone, building new worlds – like cutting my mum's old saree for a top and skirt to be sewn.

Every molecule is brought together by life's alchemist, turning raw elements into the gold of creation, constructing the formless into something magnificent.

But take heed: a creator's task isn't simple. Just as anabolism demands more than will, it consumes the very essence of life – like a craftsman pouring sweat into every stroke, shaping the world with the strength of a hundred hands. The reaction itself is a powerful force of transformation.

Suddenly, I'm aware of every cell in my body working to build me up in this intricate balance of ideation. I'm reminded of sitting to paint.

As I sit in silence to weave my thoughts, I marvel at the burning heat of energy and effort it took for all creation – in every stroke of a thoughtful note, every breath I hold, allowing intricacy to find its new home. I marvel at the thought of me –a creation.

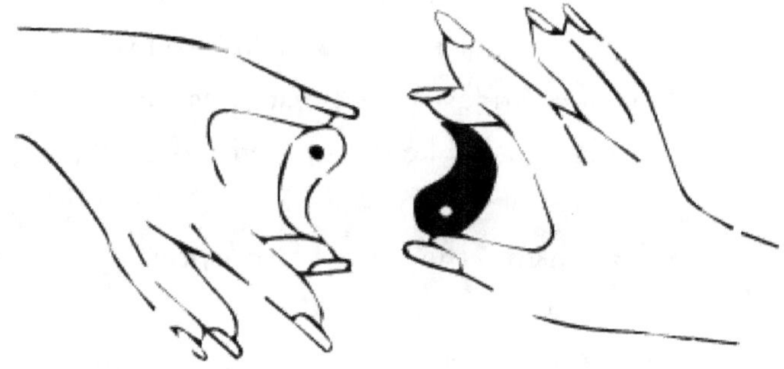

Destruction

A raging fire consuming everything in its wake, ravenous and devouring, leaving a canvas of ash where once life painted its vivid hues.

For nothing withstands the power of time; what is will turn to was, and what was will fade like memories in shades of blue.

What once was is now broken into fragments, like clues. In fast-paced reactions, entire worlds vanish, like the sudden flicker of a fuse.

Catabolism – the destructive aspect of metabolism.

Like suffering that produces perseverance, every breakdown releases energy.

Like waves crashing against cliffs, breaking them down slowly, eroding the past with the tide of inevitability, all complex molecules are reduced to simpler ones for the body's feasibility. As exothermic reactions release their energy, a byproduct now fuels important cellular functions. This is

testament that the old self must die for the new to emerge as life sanctions.
Like a potter crumbling wet clay on his wheel to restart, every destructive moment must return to beginnings, find purpose and chart a new course.
All molecules break down swiftly to ensure growth emerges, turning the largest of forms into simpler beings.
I confess I find myself reflecting on demolition; I find hope in this process yet wonder – how much it takes to create, but how little it requires to desecrate. With hope and vision, every ending can inspire a new masterpiece. In destroying parts of ourselves that no longer serve, we give into life to recreate.

Intersection

Like a sculptor's chisel, creation adds layer
upon layer, akin to an anabolic process, while
destruction chips away, much like a catabolic
process, at what is unnecessary – each
contributing to its final form.
Like a phoenix rising from its ashes, these
opposites move in cycles of new life. Within
its intertwined routes lies the in-between
path we must tread carefully to discover a life
that enriches.
Be warned, for every action to build takes
time and effort, whereas every action to
destroy requires just one move –
Like the last act of a Jenga tower.

Order and Chaos

In the erratic flashes of lightning and the roaring of thunder, I find a rhythm that resembles a heartbeat. Like the warmth of a steady hand guiding me through narrow and busy streets, I find chaos in the absence of order, but I also find them intertwined quite closely. And I realise: what I see is purely dependent on my perception of reality.
Like the branching of rivers and blood vessels that seem random and chaotic but form systems of fractal geometry, or like a trader

navigating through the volatility of the stock market finding order in numbers influenced by economic psychology – both order and chaos run rampant with each other, like the emotions felt after an apology.
Just as fractals reveal patterns within apparent randomness, so too does a football game seem chaotic until one steps onto the field and witnesses the precision beneath the motion.

To me, a game of football is chaos on a field, with a rule of order in there somewhere that I cannot perceive. But to my friend playing on that field, every move and run is a crafted order waiting for scores to be achieved. If every player is aware and aligned, order falls into place. But if coordination is amiss, even with one, it becomes a chaotic chase. The same game to me is like leaves scattered by the wind, creating art out of randomness – what pattern will form next in this unpredictable commotion? To him, it's the delicate mechanism of a Swiss watch – tiny gears moving in perfect harmony. If any gear faltered, what would be the cost of that disruption?

To me, going through every day is merging into my chaos. But to my dear friend, a day-to-day life filled with order and chaos is a perfect blend. Her meticulously crafted schedules weave order through the chaos she anticipates. Time is her catalyst in this construct of opposites. As she navigates using order as her compass, she plans every detail, considering the people involved in the activity and their ability to keep time – the true chaotic complex. For me, order and chaos are malleable, but to her, they are systemic variables that are impermeable.

Like jazz that thrives on improvisation within the framework of rhythm and melody, or like the grids of Shivajinagar markets on a Sunday afternoon – structured yet filled with all kinds of movement, creating anatomies for chaos to flow through – order is the linchpin, chaos taking bold steps, unstoppable, as order forms within. Order defines what is; chaos reveals what it could be. Like the gears of a clock, chaos is the spark of innovation; order ensures its sustainability. For even within chaos, order is found – like strength within vulnerability.

MESSAGE FROM THE AUTHOR

Hey hey! If you've made it to the end of this journey — congratulations! and a big thank you from the bottom of my heart. You've just completed a deep dive into the world of dualities, colliding moments, and perhaps, some mind-bending revelations. If you've been flipping pages with a puzzled expression, chuckling at an unexpected line, or reflecting on your own life's contrasting themes, then mission accomplished.

You would have come across various analogies in these explorations—some making sense and some not—all bits and pieces of my life and the people in it. A perception of how moments collide for me every day. If you have no idea what I'm talking about, then you're probably one of those who flipped to the last page without reading through, aren't you? I see you—go back and read. JK, no pressure!

This book was a collision of thoughts, reflections, and a little chaos. If you've had your own moments of "Ah-ha!" or "Wait, what?", don't keep it to yourself. I'd absolutely love to hear how you see these dualities and what you've learned along the way. Whether you're pondering the subtle intersections of dreams and reality or just wondering if you've somehow collided with a parallel universe (don't worry, we've all been there), feel free to share your version.

You can connect with me on Instagram @_pretty_much_art— I would love to hear from you! Whether it's a reflection, a thought, or even a meme that captures the chaos within these pages, tag me—I'd be delighted to see how you've interpreted these moments. If you have your own versions of Contrary Collisions, I'm all for it. I believe creativity is meant to be shared—not just for the sake of sharing, but like words that form sentences and sentences that go on to build great stories. Different creative thoughts should collide to shape a larger vision.

If you've enjoyed this book, or even if you've simply survived it, don't forget to give me a shout-out (or a shout-down, whichever feels right). Let's keep this dialogue going — after all, colliding moments is all about connections, right? So, pretty please? ;)

www.ingramcontent.com/pod-product-compliance
Lightning Source LLC
LaVergne TN
LVHW021213200726
843509LV00012B/1433